CARAVAGGIO TIMES TWO

S.P. SOMTOW

DIPLODOCUS PRESS
LOS ANGELES · BANGKOK · 2013

CARAVAGGIO TIMES TWO

by S.P. Somtow

Entire text © 2013 by Somtow Sucharitkul

SPECIAL EDITION
for the world premiere of
LUX IN TENEBRIS
Bangkok, Dec 6, 2013

The novelette "Chiaroscuro" previously appeared
in different form as part of the novel *Valentine: Return to Vampire
Junction* published in 1991 by Gollancz

Diplodocus Press
48 Sukhumvit Soi 33
Bangkok 10119

ISBN: 978-1-940999-04-3

0 9 8 7 6 5 4 3 2 1

SIGNATURE PAGE

No.　　/100

All proceeds from this special
edition are being donated to the
Bangkok Opera Foundation

a registered nonprofit
cultural and educational
entity

LUX
in
TENEBRIS

lyrics for a dramatization
of the life and works of
Caravaggio in music, dance,
poetry, and image

by S.P. Somtow

premiered on December 6, 2013

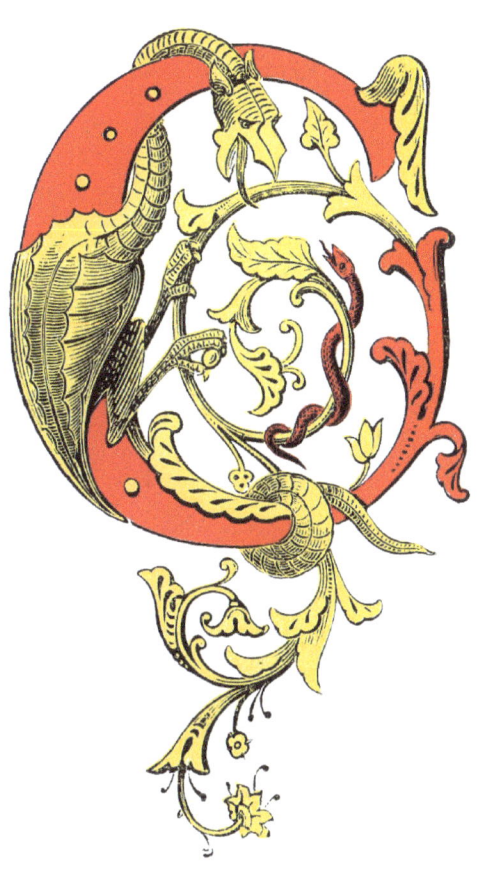

I

oscuro
chiaro
oscuro
chiaro
oscuro

II

before the universe
there was darkness
before God spoke
there was darkness
and when God has ceased to speak
darkness will come again

it is against,
in front of,
regardless of,
in despite of,
in terror of,
without fear of,
and finally,
in full embrace of
darkness
that we live

thus it is
that I stand before you

a man who has wrested
the minute particles of light
from an all embracing dark
and squeezed them together
until they became
as the glint of sunlight
on a sword that banishes darkness

I have stolen fire
from the gods
I am Prometheus
and the eagle that devours me daily
is the same eagle
on whose wings
Ganymede flew into the arms of God

III

oscuro
chiaro
oscuro
chiaro
oscuro

IV

street boys
in the dark alley
against the guttering flame

they move
they shift
swift as lizards,
angling for comfort
against the stucco

is this love?
si, signore,
if you would call it so

the flashing of my eyes
reflects the glint of coin
reflects the single shaft of moon

your *scudi* shield my soul
behind
in darkness
I am still innocent

the night was my mother
the darkness was my womb

clink clink
against wet stone
you dropped your *scudo*
in your haste to couple
and I too dropped my shield
and let you see
I have a soul
you see

V

oscuro
chiaro
oscuro
chiaro
chiaroscuro
chiaroscuro

VI

flesh firmed in the fire of poverty
lips bruised by brutal love
you I bring into my studio
you I place
your limbs, your torso
against the source of light

and so you are someone else now,
naked
embracing a ram's horns,
not a man's thorn!
you look away
though I tell you
move, move into the light
but you do not

the shadow that hides your face
and your secret parts
is me
holding the brush
and all your secrets
between my fingers

VII

chiaroscuro
chiaroscuro
chi ha?
chi ha rosa in culo?
chi ha rosa
sub rosa
sub rosa nella curia
la curia
curiosa
oscura
ra
a

VIII

the curia speaks
with the voice of God
and the cardinal flies
down from the mountain
to commission me
I am to be a messenger

and the voice says
Michelangelo,
let the faithful see
a beautiful saint
upon the wall
but let *me* see
a wanton boy

do not think,
Michelino, says the voice,
that we are lying
to the faithful
the little saint is lying
true, but in my bed,
not in the hearts
of those who truly
believe

believe, you ask me,
Micheluccio?
you dare to question me,
a prince of the high church,
a member of the curia?

look at your handiwork and learn
how light and dark
are intertwined
like lovers,
like the sun and moon,
like good and evil:

curia, curia,
curiosa....

IX

Listen
an angel calls me
an old man at a writing desk
an angel
hanging by an invisible thread
from the lips of God
and angel who strangely resembles
the urchin I had last night
in an blind alley

O it is I who have been blind
not to have known
the angel in the angle
of the light
the eternal in the infernal
the charismatic in the charisma
the lips of the divine
on the lips of sin

look down now from the sky
as you looked up in the alley
into my eyes
brazen, unrepentant.
heaven or hell?
I am still caught in between

X

oscuro
oscuro
oscuro
oscuro
os
os

XI

the sword thrusts
the head flies
the phlegm spews
one cries out
the lancet cry
is a flash in the night

killing and sex
are much the same
though death
in this case
is somewhat less
impermanent

XII

oscuro
in Latin too we say
ós cúro
I care for the bone
ósculo
I kiss
osculo culum

XIII

I am an old man looking at a skull

maybe I was a boy once
skulking in an alley
and my old customer
has gone before me
into dust

maybe I'm the customer
now old and impotent
who has seen the boys
evanescent, laughing
in the face of death
fall earlier than me,
victims of disease
and violence

maybe this is the man
I stabbed to death
in a quarrel
who still haunts me
after so much time

or

maybe I am a saint
who contemplates
a memento mori
and thinks of dust
and beyond dust,

to redemption

XIV

If you're so strong
get off that cross
if you're so great
rip out those nails
stitch back the hide
that the flagellum flayed
repair the gaping darkness
and return the world
to light

you can't
you can't
and nor can I

I've run and run and run
I won't escape
the death that waits for me

for every inch of light so fiercely won
becomes a mile of darkness
in the end

love with a languid smile
once vanquished me
but the night swallows even love,
even God

and so you hang there,
you persistent saint,
speaking of redemption
daring the Romans to let you down

you pray for the miracle of death
knowing full well
that to die on the cross
would be no miracle
that it is life
that is the miracle

Oh if you love me
get off that cross
carry me up to the tree
that overlooks your kingdom
and nail me up beside you
my pain will light the world

XV

oscuro
oscuro
chiaro
chiaro
chiaro

PART TWO

CHIAROSCURO

a novelette
about the encounter between
Caravaggio and a vampire

from the *Vampire Junction* sequence

S.P. Somtow

1991

A HISTORICAL NOTE:

The following novelette is an excerpt from *Valentine,* the sequel to my 1984 novel *Vampire Junction.* Although the novel is set in the rock-and-roll and movie milieu of 1990s Southern California, there are a number of flashbacks to the earlier lives of Timmy Valentine, the twelve-year-old rock star protagonist who became a vampire during the destruction of Pompeii in an arcane sex magic ritual in which he was castrated by two shamans who were seeking immortality.

In *Chiaroscuro* the setting is Rome of the early seventeenth century. The characters of Caravaggio and Cardinal del Monte are based on history, and though there are numerous details of my own invention, the lifestyle of this cardinal's inner circle, with its orgiastic meetings, sexual deviancy, and corruption, is well attested. It is also a fact that Caravaggio's well known painting, *The Martyrdom of Saint Matthew,* contains almost an entire painting underneath with a radically different structure. X-ray photographs show a nude angel in the front, right-hand foreground.

Out of the historical mystery of why the angel was deleted comes my fictitious inference that the angel was, in fact, the eponymous hero of my novel *Valentine.*

CHIAROSCURO

Rome, A.D. 1598-1600

Out of the first rustlings of the forest leaves come whispered words, images, odors, memories in stark chiaroscuro.
... gutted, the Colosseum rears up over the makeshift shelters of the homeless ... a full moon ... Corinthian columns matted with decaying leaves ... the heat heavy in the moist air, a rank perfume of cloves and rotting oranges and crushed rose petals and human sweat ...
To the boy the place has a strange familiarity, yet he cannot quite place the meld of fragrances. The night is alive. Boys with torches race down steep cobbled streets to light the way for a cardinal in a litter. The accents are familiar, but the tongue is somehow no longer Latin. How many centuries has it been since Pompeii? The boy does not know. This time he has emerged from the forest with very little memory at all. He has slept for a hundred years or more. The dirt of centuries crusts his eyes. He is still of the night, of the forest.
He runs behind the chair as it weaves through unlit alleys. The litterbearers do not notice him. They see a dark creature, perhaps a cat, sniffing at their heels; they do not know he smells their very blood as it races in their veins. The night is humid and the cardinal heavy; the smell of age and sweat is ill disguised by perfume and incense, and his blood is sluggish. Curious, the vampire creeps closer. He springs into the litter, blending swiftly into the ermine fringe of the cardinal's cloak. The blood oozes in this man's veins. It does not tempt. It is tainted with alcohol and unwholesome diseases. Wine dribbles from his lips.
The cardinal closes the drapes of the litter. Leaning back against cushions of velvet and damask, he reaches into his cassock and masturbates. Catlike still,

the vampire scurries behind folds of drapery. There is candlelight. Grotesque shadows against the curtains. The cardinal sighs and drinks more wine.

"Ah," says the cardinal, *"peccavi, peccavi, semper peccavi."*

Should he feed? the cat thinks. But the thirst is still dull in him.

The road is bumpy. The cardinal's silver goblet falls from his hand and grazes the cat. He remembers how silver once sapped his strength. Now it seems to have lost its power. A crucifix, studded with amethysts, dangles from a chain around the cardinal's neck. No magic emanates from it. A bible, silver-clasped, with a cruciform intaglio set into its spine, casts no spell either. Have the symbols of religion have lost their ability to harm me? he thinks. There is something different about the world. He cannot tell whether it is himself — whether the unremembered trauma that sent him to seek refuge in the forest has inured him to the powers of light and darkness — or whether it is the world that has changed during the time he has spent in the womb of the forest — whether faith has been sucked from it, like blood from the throat of a beautiful woman.

Or it is both: the magic draining from the world, the light seeping into the forest of the soul.

They come to a stop.

The cardinal adjusts his clothing. He wipes away the last drops of semen with a fold of the cassock. He crosses himself. He kisses the crucifix. He places his hat on his head and whisks aside the drapes. The cat leaps out onto marble.

A forest of feet: the sandaled feet of the litterbearers, the dirt ground in, rank; the feet of attendants, stockinged and gartered; the feet of the cardinal, his boots fringed with dead animals's fur. Cold. The marble stealing the warmth from his paws. Row upon row of candles in the distance; an altar boy slouches past, swinging a censer. The legs are all stock still, standing to attention, except for two that shift neurotically from side to side. He darts between the feet. Whispers and murmurs everywhere. As his senses become attuned to the vastness of the chamber, he hears from somewhere far away, the voice of a lone chorister, singing the same phrase over and over to himself: *Miserere mei, miserere mei.* The shuffling of feet and the rustling of vestments and the mutterings and coughs all meld into one cacophonous echo. It is a cathedral, but one so vast his head spins when he looks up.

"His Eminence," says one voice, piercing the hubbub "Cardinal del Monte."

He sees the cardinal, bloated as the setting sun, making the sign of the cross through the incense mist. His eyes are smarting from the fragrance. He slips away, his paws sliding on the cold smooth marble. He follows the music.

Miserere mei....

He focuses his mind on that musical phrase. Music is the one thing he can still grasp. Furtively he moves toward its source. There is an oak door, but it is simple enough for him to wriggle past the threshold where countless feet have worn a hollow in the stone.

He is in a vestry. Cassocks and surplices hang on pegs. The room is drafty yet windowless. The smell of children's sweat pervades the air. The singing comes from a boy who is buttoning his cassock. The voice is a boy's yet not a boy's; the boy's face is smooth, yet the eyes betray some ancient pain. He is older than he looks, the vampire thinks. He too has had his manhood ripped away. In the service of music. We do have something in common, he thinks, though he is only mortal. How they strive to prolong the transient, these humans, though all must end in dust.

Perhaps I can show him my true shape, he thinks, and already he is resolving out of the incense and the dancing dust-motes, naked as when he emerged from the forest. The dirt of death still clings to him, but he shakes it loose. Boldly he takes a cassock and surplice from one of the pegs and begins to put it on.

"Oh," says the other boy. "I didn't know there was someone here."

"People say I'm quiet," says the vampire.

"You must be new around here. I haven't seen you before, but if we don't hurry we'll both be late and we'll get whipped." For the first time the vampire notices a streak of dried blood on the back of the chorister's cassock. "My name is Guglielmo; who are you?"

He thinks quickly. What names has he overheard in the streets? "Ercole," he says, "Ercole Serafini."

"Hercules! What a name for such a pretty boy." Guglielmo laughs. "I'll call you Ercolino. You must have come with Cardinal del Monte."

"How did you know?"

"His Eminence always goes for looks before talent. I'll bet he bought you for twenty scudi from some old peasant in Naples ... you've been freshly castrated too I should think ... I can still see the pain of it in your eyes."

"*Neapolis* ... yes, Naples." Is is true , Ercolino thinks, that I once lived in that part of Italy. He does not tell Guglielmo that it was fifteen hundred years ago, in a city long since buried beneath the brimstone of Vesuvio.

"Put on this ruff," Guglielmo says, tossing him one from a chest. It is heavily starched and presses to tight against his neck. "And hurry."

"Where are we going?"

"Vespers at the Capella Sistina ... haven't they told you *anything?* Then a private party at the cardinal's in honor of the visiting Prince of Venosa — there's a pervert for you! We're to appear *travestiti* there — I hope they can find women's clothes to fit you. Do you sit on the *decani* side or the *cantores?*"

"Don't know."

"*Decani* then. That way you can stand next to me, on the south side of the nave. And you can avoid being noticed by Ser Caravaggio."

"Ser —"

"Michelangelo da Caravaggio. A mad painter who's the cardinal's pet monkey at the moment. If he catches sight of you he'll want you to pose. Something pornographic I'm sure, though there'll be some religious excuse for the subject matter. If he wants to paint you, you take his money but tell him to keep his poxy hands away from your delicate flesh." Guglielmo crosses himself.

"I'll remember," says Ercolino softly.

Guglielmo leans down and wipes a patch of dirt from his cheek with his finger. He snatches his hand away. *"Maledetto!* Cold!" he says, blowing on his finger. "You've been down into the mausoleum, all that marble, those freezing sculptures of dead popes, they have sucked the life from you...."

Ercolino smiles sadly.

"Would you like to look in the mirror before we go?" Guglielmo says.

"No ... thank you ... I don't like mirrors."

"Come on then. There's over a mile of corridors to run down before we reach the chapel.".

He stares upward from the decani choir stalls to the finger of God, the still center of the arc of the ceiling of the Capella Sistina, the moment of creation. Guglielmo whispers in his ear that eighty years ago a man named Buonarroti spent years painting that ceiling flat on his back. The boy continues to stare even though they are all kneeling, eyes downcast, murmuring the paternoster.

Our Father? he thinks. Surely not *my* father.

The boy gazes upward at the face of God. Is it only the painter's artifice, or has God changed so much during the time the vampire slept? Is that not a human God, who bears more than a passing family resemblance to Adam? Ercolino thinks: they are reflected in each other, God and man. This is a new thought for him. If even the highest, the most remote of supernatural beings, has become a little human, has the same thing happened to him? For the spirit that breathes life into the boy who calls himself Ercolino Serafini itself draws life from the collective terror in men's hearts.

I have seen God so many times, he thinks. I saw him in the eruption of Vesuvius, in the eyes of the statue of Capitoline Jove, in Bluebeard's madness and in countless icons and crucifixes, a creature conceived in pain. Other people's father, not mine. How is this God different? Could I have been bewitched by the dead hand of Buonarroti?

The choir rises. The boys cluster around an illuminated part-book which contains the notes for Prince Gesualdo's music. Ercolino is shorter than the others and squeezes in close to the parchment. A giant candle drips hot wax onto the page. He is unfamiliar with this method of notation, but it is not difficult for him to understand its principles. But as the music starts — it is the *Magnificat* — he gasps at its audacity. The melodic lines are twisted and fantastical. The harmonies are alien and abrupt. It is music that transforms itself before it can be grasped, and its eerie chords hang in the air, echoes clashing against echoes, like a series of unfinished sculptures....

Who can have written such music? It is not a perfect music. It is a music of anguish and uncertainty ... it is a *human* music. Again the vampire wonders whether it is he who has changed, or the world.

On their knees once more for a set of *responsoria,* he whispers to Guglielmo: "This Prince of Venosa, this Gesualdo — can you point him out to me?"

Guglielmo directs his gaze toward the altar, where there is a section reserved for the college of cardinals. Among the figures robed in crimson is a man dressed all in black. He seems sullen. He is fidgeting. Perhaps his own music has disturbed him. "They say he murdered his wife when he discovered her *in flagrante* with another man," Guglielmo says.

"Strangled her!" says another boy gleefully from the pew above.

"Nonsense — he ran her through with his sword — cut off the other man's balls, too," says Guglielmo. "And by the way, I'm sorry I said you had no talent. I'll never be a man, but I'm man enough to admit it when I'm wrong. You're well named, Serafini."

But Ercolino is not listening. His gaze has shifted to the man kneeling next to the mad composer. He is unkempt; he stares from side to side; his doublet does not match his cloak, and his left stocking is torn. He wonders who the man is, how he could be up there among the cardinals; he does not appear in the least bit embarrassed by his shabbiness.

"Don't look at *him!*" Guglielmo whispers urgently.

Too late. They have seen each other.

They rise for a reading from the *Book of Revelation.* It is a curious, stilted, ungrammatical Latin, he thinks, for he remembers well the severe cadence of that tongue as it was uttered by the pleasure-seekers at Baiae and the doomed denizens of Pompeii and the courtiers from the palace of the Emperor Titus.

"Look away!" Guglielmo says. "Nothing good will come of your attracting the notice of Ser Caravaggio!"

They look into each other's eyes. The boy knows what the man sees: a child, malleable, a sheet of virgin parchment — mortals have always seen him this way. He does not look away. The music begins again — it is the hymn *Ave Maris Stella.* Ercolino does not join in. He has smelled blood. Something has awakened the hunger, dormant so long. It is something about the man.

Suddenly he realizes why the man is so dishevelled. He has come from a brawl. His arm is crudely bandaged with strips of linen torn from a shirt. The blood is fresh and pungent. The odor slices through the incense and the scented wax. It is irresistable. The paean to the virgin swells; the voices of the choristers tremble with that hopeless passion only eunuchs can muster. But the cardinals are nodding off and the altarboys are half-drugged by the incense; it seems to Ercolino that only he and Caravaggio are truly alive at the moment. No time passes between desire and its fulfillment. Ercolino transforms himself into a fine mist and is wafted toward the painter amid clouds of incense. The man continues to stare at where Ercolino stood. But he is already at Ser Caravaggio's side, ripping at the bandages with his cat-claws, for all the painter can see is a dark furry creature lapping the lifeblood from his wounded arm. He closes his eyes. He smiles. He knows it's me, Ercolino thinks. He *knows!*

He feeds now. Blood spilled in violence tastes sweetest; sourest is the blood of the bedridden. This is an angry blood, a blood full of the spices of heightened emotions; it is the blood of an artist. The vampire exults. The warmth floods him. He drinks deep. He tears at the flesh, he thrusts his cat's tongue deep into riven muscle. Caravaggio murmurs. He utters a single sharp cry of pain or ecstacy and then snaps out of his rêverie. He has ejaculated. He moves his hand to cover the stain on his codpiece. The incense masks the smell of semen, but the vampire can smell it even through the intoxicating fragrance of fresh blood. The painter glances shiftily about him. The cardinals are snoring; Gesualdo is scribbling on a scrap of parchment.

Caravaggio laughs out loud. The cat mews and leaps off his arm, nestling between the brocade of his jacket and the dark oiled wood.

"Who are you?" says the painter. There is wonder in his eyes. Has the illusion slipped? Has Caravaggio seen his true form? He wrenches himself back into the catshape. He gazes up into the painter's eyes. He stares past those eyes into the eyes of God the Father.

I am a cat, he thinks. *I am a cat.* He does not think Caravaggio is convinced. How can that be? A few times, an innocent has been able to see through the illusion. A child who has not learned to separate the inner and the outer worlds

— a village idiot perhaps — these are the only humans capable of seeing his true form. They, and the beasts of the forest in whose shapes he cloaks himself. He knows that the painter is not an innocent.

The cat retreats into the fog of incense. Panicking, he springs from the pew and swirls into the mist, resolving himself once more at the side of Guglielmo, picking up the *Ave Maris Stella* in mid-phrase, melding seamlessly into the arc of the music.

Without looking back he knows that the man is still staring at him.

I'm afraid, he thinks. I don't want to look back. When you drink someone's blood, there's a bond. It is the bond of hunter and prey, the love-death dance of the world. But with this man I don't know if I'm hunting or hunted. I'm afraid, he thinks.

But at last, with the borrowed life-force racing in his veins and lending him the illusion of warmth, he gives himself up to the music. The music soars. It is the music that allows him to pretend he has not lost his soul.

He sings.

The apartments of Cardinal del Monte: the announced entertainment is a masque penned by the celebrated poet Torquato Tasso. The boys are to appear only in the fourth act, as a chorus of odalisques, for the setting of the play is the seraglio of a Turkish pasha, and the plot, such as it is, concerns the efforts of Dionysus, a Greek mage, to rescue his beloved Francesca from concubinage and a fate worse than death. It slowly becomes clear that the performance is in fact a vicious parody of the poet's work, and that some wag has simply taken the noble Tasso's drama *Aminta* and cleverly turned it into a trivial tale by changing the names and bastardizing the rhymes. Double-entendres abound, as do references to Cardinal del Monte's none too secret fondness for the Turkish vice of sodomy.

Guglielmo and Ercolino have donned some androgynous tunics which bear little resemblance to the actual dress of Turkish harem girls. They have wreaths in their hair. They are there to mingle with the cardinal's guests. There are few women. There are many princes of the church, reclining on plump silken couches or sprawling across the floor like scarlet tents. There are dandies. There is a withered duchess whose face has been powdered to a marmoreal whiteness. The conversation is carried on in whispers and titters. Now and then one of the guests looks about him warily. They seem to live in terror of some scandal.

The walls are covered with artwork, but all of it is concealed with drapes. There are statues too, but they too are covered up. The apartment smells of the oranges stuffed with cloves that the rich carry on their persons whenever they must venture out into the streets, to sniff whenever the stench of putrefaction becomes too suffocating.

Cardinal del Monte sits on an overstuffed throne, a page boy on his lap. The boy is singing to the accompaniment of a theorbo. He cannot keep in tune because the masque musicians, sawing away at their viols from the next room, are in a different key. No one is watching the masque anyway, except for Prince Gesualdo, who squats on a stool with a bottle of wine in his hand.

"They'll be going on till dawn!" Guglielmo whispers in Ercolino's ear. "But with any luck, after we muddle through our little production number, we can slip away. I know a good shortcut to the choristers' dormitory."

"I can't stay until dawn," Ercolino says. He hopes he will not have to explain.

The cardinal is laughing. The throne's legs squeak against the marble as he shifts his bulk. *"Per bacco,"* he shouts, "the ancient Romans with their orgies were never as decadent as we!" The audience claps as though his utterance were a veritable pearl. But Ercolino thinks: If only they had seen what I have seen. After fifteen hundred years, the past seems more present than ever. "More wine!" the cardinal shrieks, "and after we have become very, very drunk, perhaps a peek at my secret paintings!"

Collective gasping in the audience. The secret paintings are what they have really all come to see. Ercolino sees Guglielmo chuckling to himself.

"Why, what is in those paintings?" Ercolino asks him.

"Street urchins masquerading as heroic figures of myth and scripture," says Guglielmo, "and all, of course, without a stitch of clothing. Oh, there are nymphs as well as shepherds; the cardinal knows his own tastes, but he has something for everybody."

Coyly Guglielmo adjusts the folds of his tunic so as to conceal as much as can be hidden with so skimpy a sheet of cloth. He straightens the wreath in his hair. He makes an attractive girl, Ercolino thinks, when he does not try to walk; his stride betrays him. Ercolino himself, though he has kohled his eyes and stuck a blood-red rose behind his ear, he feels no need to play the part of a woman. What is man or woman? he thinks. I am not even human.

Soon it will be dawn. The boy vampire has not yet slept since his emergence from the forest. He does not think the dawn will pain him as much as it used to. He is becoming inured to his own superstitions.

Cardinal del Monte has waddled off his throne. He has yanked the first curtain aside to reveal a startling Cupid, large as life . Attendants raise their candelabra. This is a brazen Cupid — one of the grubby children of the street, scrubbed clean and sporting a pair of ill-fitting wings. The child, still scrubbed, is right there — he is the one who has been sitting on the cardinal's lap. He giggles.

Another painting — the onlookers ooh and aah — depicts the blind prophet Teiresias as he gazes on the unholy coupling of serpents — the impiety, as the myth goes, causing him to sprout breasts and cursing him to live as a woman until the spell can be broken. Unable to control themselves at the sight, two of the cardinal's guests begin to couple themselves right there at the foot of the painting.

Cardinal del Monte trots off into the next chamber, where the depictions are still lewder. On a wall-sized canvas, an orgy is in progress; in one corner, a man in a flowing robe — an Israelite — views the scene with an expression of disgust; two *putti* hover around his shoulders, whispering into his ears. A muscular, winged youth stands beside him, brandishing a bejeweled sword.

"Ah," Guglielmo says, laughing, "the patriarch Lot and the Archangel Michael prophesying destruction to the Sodomites. The biblical subject justifies including the orgy."

"I see." He does not want to say that the orgy seems rather tame by comparison to what he witnessed during the heyday of the Empire. In fact, the proceedings at the cardinal's affair seem listless, the decadence selfconscious and contrived. He loses interest as del Monte moves on, whisking aside arrases lifting draperies. He is like an overgrown child, Ercolino thinks, this prince of the church.

He remembers a scene from the circus at Pompeii — a Christian being crunched in the jaws of a lioness. Others burned alive, crucified, raped to death by jackasses ... this is what they died for, he thinks. It is they who now rule in Rome ... and this is what they have become.

Inwardly he laughs. Perhaps the world is not so changed as he thought. Perhaps it is only me after all, he thinks. His mind floats ... he finds he has drifted unawares once more into the shape of the black cat.

It is good, he thinks. Good to forget being human, to partake once more of the forest.

The drunken laughter now comes from far overhead as he slinks across the costly Persian carpet stained with wine. In one room choirboys are giggling as they apply the feminine makeup of the odalisques. One room is empty save for a naked woman, pouting, in a copper bathtub. There is a corridor lined with busts and broken statues that seem to have been plundered from all the sacred places of the ancients. One room is hung with threadbare tapestries depicting the deeds of saints and sinners. A massive bronze Jupiter gazes down from a niche and he cannot help mewing a prayer in a half-forgotten language.

From behind a curtain he can hear a man singing softly to himself. *Miserere mei.* It is the same lilting strain he first heard from the lips of Guglielmo. He slithers past velvet into an inner room. Caravaggio is there. He is painting. A huge canvas dominates one end of the chamber, which is lit by row upon row of scented candles, like a church. The canvas is dark save for shafts of light that illumine the figures in the foreground. He sees St. Matthew, thrown onto the ground and about to be slain. His killer hunkers above him. A boy shrieks out in terror, while overhead, riding a whirlwind, angels watch, their faces impassive. Other figures are crudely blocked out.

Caravaggio works with profound concentration. He is clearly in terrible pain. He does not hear the mangled verse of Torquato Tasso or the jangle of the theorbo and the off-key choirboy. He is absorbed. He paints with deft flicks of the wrist, working one tiny area — the flesh-tones of a screaming child's face — over and over in infinitesimal gradations of color.

He still has not changed his clothes, and his blood is still dripping from his wound onto the marble. Blood runs onto his palette and streaks the pigments. He grimaces. Yet his wrist moves swiftly — it dances across the canvas to a music that the boy vampire can almost hear — the tortuous music of Carlo Gesualdo — the music of hell, the hell God made.

The hot blood wakes his hunger. Catlike he pounces. His paws slip along smooth marble till his tongue tastes blood again. Blood races through him like fire. Blood warms him into simulated life. He purrs.

As though in a dream the painter says: "Why do you stand over my shoulder? Have you come for me? Are you the angel of death?" Illusion is useless. The man has the power to see his true self. It is the same gift that has made him a painter, and the same gift that has made him mad.

"No, Ser Caravaggio, I am not the angel of death. I am Ercole Serafini, sir; I am a decani soprano of the papal choir." Only when he utters these words does he realize that this must be his new identity for a little while. The world has become more vast as well as more human. He must stay inside this microcosm until he has learned the new rules. "My friends call me Ercolino," he adds.

"Oh, beautiful and terrifying. Oh, but your eyes say so much more than do your lips. You are more than another one of del Monte's singing boys, bought from the slums, gelded by a cut-rate barber. I have seen you in dreams." He becomes animated. His eyes shine with passion and madness. "If I could only capture you on this canvas ... perhaps I'd be less afraid then." And he has not even looked at Ercolino yet! He has only seen him ... reflected in the oil of the painting, perhaps ... a reflection of one who can cast no reflection! Unless he is speaking to a creature of his imagination, an angel of his dementia.

"Why are you afraid?" Ercolino says.

He puts down his paintbrush for a moment. "Oh, it is the fever," he says. Beneath the tangle of beard, Ercolino can see that the skin is soaked with sweat and cracked and caked with pus. Caravaggio is ill. His blood is almost at boiling point. It is a sweet blood, made tart by the ineffective possets of the cardinal's resident quack.

"So much darkness," the boy says, looking at the painting. "And the light, painfully bright."

"But life itself is *chiaroscuro*," says the painter, "a perpetual darkness leavened only by the lightning of love, inspiration, agony."

"You're not at the revels with all the other guests, Ser Caravaggio? I've been told you're a lover of pleasure, a sensual man."

"Oh, no. They keep me here, the trained monkey, the caged artist. What would I do at the party? Oh, but they love my crude ways. I am so entertaining. Tell me, boy, when you sing, don't you feel like a whore?"

"I don't know."

"Well, just look at you!" He turns to the boy vampire. His blood stains the boy's lips. How strange I must look, the boy thinks, in my preposterous costume, a sexless creature radiating the sexuality of a borrowed gender. "Ah," Caravaggio says, "but you *are* the death-angel I've been dreaming of. You must come to my studio in the morning; I'll pay you half a scudo a week for your pains, until the picture is done. And meals, of course; His Eminence has supplied me with an excellent cook until such time as the *Martyrdom* is done."

"I can only come at night," says Ercolino, "and I won't need food."

"No, of course not," says the painter. "But can man live on blood alone?" He does not smile, but his eyes hint of mirth and irony.

"I can."

"But soon my wound will heal."

"You will have other wounds."

"Yes."

He hears the strains of the ode of the odalisques from the cardinal's private theater. "I must go," he says. He backs away, unwilling to look away from the

unfinished painting. Its beauty is yet unborn; it is a cadaver with no heart, no blood, like a hungry vampire on a dark street corner.

"Give me the rose," says the painter. "A pledge." Unasked, he plucks it from the boy's hair. A thorn jabs his finger. Blood spurts; he seems to relish the pinprick. If the boy does not go soon he will have to feed again. The hunger is always there.

The boy escapes, transforms, darts through the mass of satiated flesh toward the candlelit theater to take his place with the choir of unmanned youths. The song of the odalisques is silly and though he has never rehearsed it it is simple enough for him to join in in the monotonous refrain:

Amor, amor, amor,
Vittorioso amor.

A single swath of brightness sweeps across darkness. Ercolino stands half in and half out of the light. False wings sprout from his shoulders. He cannot see the painter's face. Only the rapid motion of the brush, shadow dancing against the far wall, the plaster peeling, a cockroach circling a wine bottle.

But now and then he hears Ser Caravaggio's voice, whispering to himself: *my love, my death.* He wonders what the painter means. The man will not let him see the canvas. The boy stands in the light and the shadow. He does not feel the cold because he is himself the source of the cold. It is high summer and a hot wind blows from Ostia and the stench hangs heavy over the sewer outside the window. But the room is cool. The boy holds a pose of marmoreal stillness; the feathers shiver, but he does not; he does not even breathe; a rancid sweetness hangs in the air; a dew has formed on his pearl-smooth skin; his eyes are innocent of feeling.

The shadow of the paintbrush moves feverishly back and forth along the wall. *My love, my death* — what do those things mean?

"Do you know why you cannot see me in mirrors?" says Ercole Serafini.

"No, tell me," says the painter from behind the canvas.

"Because I am myself a mirror. Of myself I am nothing. When you look at me, you see only yourself, your shadow-half, the part you do not wish to see."

"Philosophy," says Ser Caravaggio, "don't speak to me of philosophy. I get enough of that from those fucking cardinals. Philosophy is the handmaiden of sodomy." He flings his paintbrush across the floor. He downs a quarter of the flagon in a single gulp, cockroach and all.

The boy has not even breathed.

"Why do you call me the angel of death?" he asks the painter. "I am no angel, and I am not death."

"Don't speak to me! I'm making the lightning dart across your eyes. I'm making your glance arc over the dying saint toward the portrait of myself I have put in, peeking timorously from an alcove. No, don't say a word. Don't move. Don't even breathe. Be. *Be.*"

He has come to the painter's apartments every night. Every night he has drawn a little blood, just enough to take the edge off his hunger; every night he has stood in the corner, half in, half out of the shadow, wearing nothing but the harness to which are attached two flightless wings. Sometimes he sings. Before dawn he returns to the dormitory where the choristers sleep, three or four to a bed; he lies, sleepless, next to the snoring Guglielmo, waiting for the bell that will summon them to breakfast and to matins; he is shunted from service to service, down dark hallways lined with ancient sculptures pilfered from the temples of pagan Greece and Rome; he never encounters the sun, though Rome in the summer is so sultry that the very stone of the walls sweats. Now and then a shaft of sunlight streams in through a chink in the ceiling, or into an atrium, or through an open window; the sunlight does not burn him any more. He has ceased to believe in good and evil; light does not kill him, night does not nurture him. He has seen too much of the darkness in men's hearts to be affected by their folly, their superstition.

In the hour before the dawn he settles on the cold marble like dew; he resolves into his familiar shape, tiptoes toward the bed. The smell of eunuchs sleeping is different from the smell that rises from the beds of whole men. The air is innocent of the pheromones of arousal or the scent of drying semen. There is a sweetness to their slumber; their sleep is the limbo of the unbaptised. Ercolino stands for a moment in a pool of twilight, not yet quite substantial. It is at that moment that Guglielmo pounces on him. When the eunuch's hands touch the icy flesh they quickly let go.

"Ercolino, Ercolino!" says the chorister. "I've been spying on you at night. Cardinal del Monte pays me. He wants to know all about you."

"You shouldn't. Sometimes it's hard to follow me."

"I've seen you go to the painter's house, the one I warned you against. I've climbed up the wall and stood on tiptoe on the shingles and seen you drink the man's blood … what does it mean? I never see you eat or drink. Ercolino, you're not human, are you?"

"Caravaggio calls me his angel of death. But that is his own imagining. I am what people make me."

"I've heard about creatures like you. You are immortal. You were here before our Lord walked the earth. When you take enough blood from a man, he becomes immortal too."

"Half-truths," says Ercole Serafini, thinking of the painter grinding his very blood into the canvas, wringing his soul into the pigment.

"I want to be immortal too, Ercolino. Make me immortal."

"You don't know what you're asking."

"But I think I do. I think you are a vampire. I think I have seen you sucking the blood from the painter's fingers as he closes his eyes in ecstacy. There is something Satanic about you. Such beauty can only come from evil, put here to tempt men. Am I wrong?"

"You don't really believe that, Guglielmo." Though the room is dark, the boy can see with the clarity of one born from darkness. To him it is as though the chamber were awash with a soft sourceless light. Guglielmo only thinks that the shadow masks his emotions. The light that comes from the shunning of light shines so fiercely that it betrays every flicker of doubt in the chorister's face. Ercolino knows that his friend has seen something; he knows he does not understand what he has seen, and that for him all is confusion and terror and the yearning half-remembered from the time before he was unmanned. Ercolino says, "I can't give it back to you."

"I don't want that back," says Guglielmo, but the boy knows he lies. "I just want to be like you. And if I can't, then I will hurt you."

"I cannot be hurt," says the boy vampire. But that has not been true for over a century.

The death-angel rears up from the shaft of radiance, his arm upraised, one finger pointing up to the sky. He is impassioned; there is a lasciviousness about his smile; the paintbrush has imbued his boyish musculature with a silky, sensuous sheen, as though it were kissed by moonlight. A line leftward from the crook of the painting touches the upraised weapon that will strike the doomed evangelist. A woman pleads, her arms reaching out toward the angels' knees; and old men look on, lugubrious and morose. To the far left, surfacing in abrupt chiaroscuro, is the face of a somber woman, her hand against her chin. Her emotions are unfathomable. Perhaps she is awed at the mystery of martyrdom; perhaps she is a little aroused at the sight of blood; perhaps, perhaps ... it is the angel she sees. Perhaps it is he who stirs, within her, longings dark and profane. For the street-urchin curl of his lip, the insolent forwardness of his demeanor, the tantalizing *vade mecum* of his gaze, surely these do not spring from the divine in him, but from the earthly; perhaps the woman is perplexed that the eunuch of heaven is imbued with such sensuality.

The boy vampire hears the pause in the nervous rhythm of brushstrokes. Caravaggio has put down his brush and steps back to admire his handiwork. The room is full of dancing, flickering light; there are candles and oil lamps everywhere. Ercolino steps away from the wings, which have been attached to a free-standing metal frame against which he has been leaning, holding the same languorous gesture for about an hour.

A heavy arras has been drawn over the chamber's bay windows, blocking the moonlight. The air in the room is stifling. The dust that dances in the dense and sodden air is peppered with powdered pigments. It is oppressive, but Caravaggio is oblivious to everything except the painting and the boy vampire.

"It is close to completion," the painter says, and drains the third wine bottle of the evening. The wine is sour and its vinegary odor pervasive. "Come, Ercolino, look at how I've immortalized you."

"But I already am immortal."

"My love, my death," Ser Caravaggio says. He always says this. Over and over he says it. "Yes, you are immortal, you beautiful child; you are immortality made flesh. Oh, it is a sin for you to be so beautiful; how can I dare to imprison such beauty in a cage of canvas, pigment, linseed oil?"

The boy laughs. "I am not imprisoned," he says.

He stands there, his expression a perfect vacuousness. He knows what the painter sees: a creature maddeningly erotic yet strangely inviolable. He sees the painter's gaze move downward from his unblinking eyes down to his unsmiling lips, the undefined musculature, the inhuman pallor of his skin, the flat and hairless pubis, the white scars of castration, the penis that cannot stiffen. Caravaggio's eyes are glazed from drunkenness and sleepless nights. The blood will be sour tonight from the alcohol, and sweet from the burning up of body fat; Ercolino smells the blood, and knows its composition intimately, as a wine-taster knows his vinyards and his vintages.

"Oh, Ercolino, I long to possess your body and yet ... why do I find myself unable even to try? ... Cardinal del Monte sends over the pick of the choirboys all the time; he hired me, you know, because I ... understand his tastes ... I've had every homeless urchin in the street for the price of an evening meal ... you, you, you ... who come here willingly ... not in fear of the Cardinal's wrath, not driven by greed or hunger ... you I dare not have. Why do I fear you so much, my angel of death?"

"I have told you, Ser Caravaggio, I'm not an angel and I'm not death."

The painter's blood is racing. Yes, he can hear its music, joyous, like the rustling of mighty wings. The hunger wakened in him is akin to passion. I must feed, he thinks. I have stood here, motionless, playing at being his dark angel, creature of his fantasies. I have told him time and again that I am not what he wants me to be. It is always this way. Always I fulfil the dream-wishes of men, sometimes even their death-wishes; I can never be perceived as anything else. Perhaps I do not even have an independent existence apart from these mortal passions, the self-destructive yearnings, that men project on to me.

Oh, that music! It is the blood, responding to the hunger; that rhapsodic and chromatic surge of life's essence, driven by the rhythm of heart; oh, I am hunger, thinks the boy vampire, hunger is all I am. Oh, I must feed, I must feed.

Caravaggio says, "I am ready. Take me, dark angel of my passion. Is that not why you've come to me ... to carry me to hell in some ecstatic transport of forbidden lust? You have already drunk my blood ... now drink my soul!"

"I don't want your soul. I only want the blood itself."

"I demand that you take my soul!" the painter screams. He turns to void his bladder into a chamberpot. "My soul!" he cries again.

And he flings himself upon the boy, whose flesh is colder than marble. The boy reflects: To him, life and art are one; both are chiaroscuro, fragments of brilliance set against vast canvases of shadow. They are at cross purposes, and yet each feeds on the other.

Ser Caravaggio tears away at his own clothing, hugs the cool flesh with an ardor that cannot be quenched; he strokes and caresses, trying to waken a response that cannot come; he is on his knees before his dark angel, who is no spirit at all but the very opposite of the spiritual, carrion imbued with the illusion of life, carrion that thirsts so much for the life force that it drinks and drinks again and yet is never sated; oh, oh, I am carrion, Ercolino thinks, and bends down to sink his canines into the painter's shoulder, making him cry out with pain that is also lust. Ser Caravaggio sweats and moans but there is that about me which prevents him from becoming hard. What does it matter? Why should it concern me, the illusion that this poor mortal has fashioned for himself? Is he not prey? Is he not just a warm teat from which to suck the life-force? Oh, but the boy vampire is troubled where he was never troubled before. The encounter with Bluebeard has changed him utterly. Not long ago, he remembers, in England, I watched Kit Marlowe bleed to death in a Deptford tavern, and I did not even feel the hunger, not in the same way as before ... the hunger was tinged with bitterness.

But here comes blood. Blood. Oh, oh, the blood ... oh, it is warm, warm, warm ... oh, it is a drug that feeds its own addition. Oh, yes, the bitterness that he has begun to feel is there too, but perhaps he is more used to it now. He tongues that gushing warmth. It tingles. It shoots into him and leaves him wanting more ... I could kill him, he thinks to himself. I could suck all of it out and still not be fulfilled. But I would kill his genius.

Caravaggio weeps. "I love you," he whispers.

What kind of love can this be? the vampire thinks. It is a pavane in which each partner dances alone. He sinks his teeth deeper into the painter's neck. His canines rend flesh now. The blood comes spurting. I must not take too much ... I must conserve ... gently ... gently ... the painter's body shudders with a terror that is like ecstacy.

They hear a tearing sound. It is the arras. It is ripped down, and two figures stand framed in the open window, one bulky and big-jowled, the other a slim and cowering.

"Shame, shame, shame, shame," says the voice of Cardinal del Monte.

"I told you, Your Eminence," says the voice of Guglielmo, "that the two of them were up to some vile perversion."

The boy looks up. His lips are blotched with crimson.

"Satanic blood-rituals," says the cardinal. "I tend to turn a blind eye at the vices of the flesh — ah, for is not flesh weak? — but heresy is another matter, isn't it, Guglielmo?" Guglielmo nods. "He has been a good spy, and well deserving of the extra scudi I have lavished on him." And the cardinal tosses him a purse, which the chorister pockets, never taking his eyes off Ercolino.

Who slowly licks from his lips the last traces of blood.

The cardinal and Guglielmo step forward. Del Monte, robed in crimson, each finger ringed with a different jewel, is shaking with hypocritical indignation; the eunuch Guglielmo looks at Ercole Serafini with trepidation and desire. Caravaggio sobs.

"You have drunk each other's blood, in savage mockery of the holy sacrament of the eucharist," the cardinal continues. "I witnessed it, and so did this boy. You're at my mercy."

Defiantly, Ercolino says, "He did not drink my blood, Your Eminence; I was the only one who drank. And not to mock the scriptures, but to fulfil a terrible need which is the curse of all my kind."

"And what *kind* might that be, boy?" says the cardinal.

Guglielmo crosses himself and looks away at last. "He promised me immortality if I would follow his dark ways ... if I would sell my soul," he says. "He is a demon." The lie does not come easily; it is wrenched from him; Ercolino feels a certain compassion for him in his confusion.

"He is an angel," Caravaggio says. "He has come to foreshadow my death."

"Vanity, vanity, all is vanity," says the cardinal. He comes forward. His blood smells of cloves and garlic.

The cardinal glares at the painting. Caravaggio steps back. Somehow he seems lost.

Ercolino sees himself. Am I really this beautiful? he asks himself. He has never seen himself since his transformation, of course, since his world contains no mirrors. He cannot even see himself reflected in Caravaggio's eyes. The

cardinal pulls a little hand-mirror from his capacious vestments and holds it up to Ercolino's face. He sees nothing, of course. He throws the mirror on the ground and the glass shatters. Then, turning to the table, covered with candles and with mixed pigments, he seizes the largest of the brushes, dips it in carmine, and proceeds to desecrate the figure of angel of death.

Caravaggio watches, stony-faced. An artist is little more than a liveried servant. He does not look away as the cardinal covers the angel's features with smears of red, as he daubs the crimson over the slender body. He takes particular pleasure in bloodying its genitalia. He laughs. He is as drunk as Caravaggio. He is as drunk with power as he is with wine. He laughs and laughs until Ercolino is afraid he will collapse in a stupor. But before he can do that, Guglielmo comes, supports him as he staggers back to the window; there is a basket and a pulley there. It must have been constructed just so the cardinal could spy on Caravaggio and play his little joke on him.

Just before he disappears, Cardinal del Monte says to Ercolino: "Go back to the gutter, *ragazzo;* we don't want any devil children in the house of God."

Gugliemo does not look into his eyes; Ercolino knows that he fears his silent reproach. If he were only to look, he thinks, he will see that I do not reproach him. They all grasp at me; when they can hold on to me, when they find me insubstantial as the air, they become angry; they turn their anger on me; even the cardinal.

The night air, muggy and oppressive, blows into the chamber. The candleflames waver and flare up.

"It is just as well," says Ercole Serafini to the painter. "I am not what you think me. Paint me out of the picture. Forget me. Let me step back into the *oscuro,* out of the beam of light."

Caravaggio seems stone sober now. He seems to be looking at the boy vampire in a completely different light. "You're right," he says. "You are no angel. You're just another one of those children of the streets, kinkier than the others, perhaps; you tricked me. I tricked myself. Go back to the gutter, boy."

"*Addio, mio signore,*" says the boy vampire softly. Then he funnels into shadow and drifts down into the street below.

#

For many years he has haunted the back alleys of the eternal city. The city is rich in prey. It has been easy for him to hide in the squalor, in the shadows; like Caravaggio's chiaroscuro, it is a city where the bright places shine with the brilliance of the sun, and the dark places are utterly dark; where the marble still gleams on the walls of the Michaelangelo's Basilica of St. Peter, where prostitutes ply their trade in the shadow of the grime-crusted walls of the Colosseum, where the marble gleams no more.

He has had many names in the intervening years. Ercolino, Andrea, Sebastian, Gualtier, Orlando. He has lured countless travelers to their death, offering to show them the ruins of the Forum Romanum or Nero's Golden House, giving them instead surcease of feeling. He has been careful to kill cleanly and permanently. He needs no companions in the twilight world that he inhabits. He contemplates eternity alone.

One evening, strolling through the marketplace, he overhears the name Caravaggio. Pausing to listen to the chatter of apprentice artists, he realizes that the *Martyrdom of Saint Matthew* has finally been completed; that tomorrow it will be unveiled at the Chiesa di San Luigi die Francesi. It is not far from the market. He is seized by a need to see what has become of the painting, which he last saw blotched by the cardinal's wrath.

His form blurs, shimmers, condenses into the familiar black cat. He races through the alley. His senses are made keen by the nature of the animal; the smell of blood is heightened. In a doorway a wounded soldier is bleeding. Inside a seedy apartment, a girl is menstruating. A child trips, skins his knee against the cobblestones. All these give off the sensual scent of blood. There is time for that later. Tonight he must see what has happened to the angel of death.

He leaps; he springs; his feet pad softly on the stones; soon he is at the Palazzo Madama, across the street from the massive portals of the church. How well he remembers that place; it housed the studio where he drank the painter's blood. Soon he has made himself into a mist and is funneling through the keyhole into the house of God. Incense and candlelight. Stillness. And there is the painting, still draped, still unseen, in a side chapel dedicated by the Contarelli family.

He has become a cat again. He sidles up to the altar, insinuates himself through the wooden railings. The shadow of the great crucifix dances in the flames of a hundred novena candles. The pain is but a pinprick as he slips in and out of the crucifix's penumbra; he has become more and more inured to it, understanding now that even the devices of the divine are stained with corruption. He leaps onto the altar. There is as yet no altarpiece. The *Martyrdom* hangs on a lateral wall. He leaps again, he scurries down the nave, he crouches at the foot of Caravaggio's painting.

He is close to the drapery; he could perhaps whisk it away with a flick of his paws, or return to human shape and simply pull down the eleven-foot-square velvet covering. But before he can make up his mind, he hears footsteps on the stone floor, echoing; he slides into a fold of the drapery; torchlight fills the chamber. It is Cardinal del Monte. He has put on weight; he leans on the shoulder of a young man ... Guglielmo.

He is glad Caravaggio is not with them.

Guglielmo has changed. Because he is a eunuch, he does not seem to have aged that much; but there is a deadness in his eyes, like that of one whose mind has been dulled by opiates. The vampire watches.

"Pull down the veil, Guglielmo! I want to see." The cardinal manages to stuff himself into a front pew. Guglielmo opens the railing and pulls aside the velvet.

At first the vampire sees nothing but a jumble. Light and darkness jigsaw across the eleven-foot-square canvas. Out of the kaleidoscope emerge faces, arms with taut musculature, wings, a plumed hat; all flicker in the candlelight; all seem in constant motion.

This is the *Martyrdom of Saint Matthew.* The angel of death no longer stands in the foreground, lit up in all his grim beauty. The painting is full of darkness. Where the angel once stood, a boy is recoiling from the scene of the saint's assassination. Here and there in the front stand naked penitents, readying themselves for baptism. There is an angel on a cloud above; the angel's face is hidden; he hands the dying saint the palm of martyrdom; all that can be seen of the angel is the crook of the arm, the taut curve of a buttock jutting from the obscure æther around the cloud; a boyish leg with its foot pointing skyward, perhaps to the face of god.

Where the woman was sitting, on the far left, there are now other figures. In the middle distance, peering from the gloom, is the face of Caravaggio himself, an observer, within yet perpetually outside the world he has created.

It is beautiful, the boy vampire thinks.

Cardinal del Monte is speaking to Guglielmo, who squats obsequiously at his feet. "That devil-child is gone from the picture now," he says. "Pity."

"Why, Your Eminence?" Guglielmo says.

"It was a pretty thing, and I like to come to churches in the middle of the night and gaze at these ... divine manifestations of beauty and ... enjoy their profane aspects. If you know what I mean."

Still in his feline shape, the vampire slithers from darkness to darkness along the cold stone floor of the *chiesa*. He sits in the cardinal's shadow. The cardinal has loosened his cassock and allowed his penis to rear up from the folds of red fabric. Mechanically, his eyes devoid of feeling, Guglielmo begins to fellate him. The cardinal gazes at the painting and sighs. "That devil-child — such a pretty thing, with such a fine voice; a pity. A pity. He could no doubt have been trained to perform your function, Guglielmo, and he might have put a little more ardor into it than you."

Guglielmo does not answer. The black cat peers into his eyes. He remembers it all now: how the young eunuch begged him to give him immortality, not understanding its dreadful consequences; how, thwarted in his plea, he told the cardinal stories of blood-rites and devil-worship; how they had parted, with the cardinal angrily defacing the canvas, with Guglielmo unable to look his old friend in the eye ... How low he has sunk now! the vampire thinks. He is an empty thing. His betrayal of me haunts him; it has made him into the cardinal's whore.

It is not so the much the casual sacrilege of it that appalls him — is he not himself, after all, a sacrilegious thing to these people, a very concretization of the dæmonic? — but the vacuousness he sees in Guglielmo. It is as though he were already dead.

An uncontrollable anger rips through him. He cannot stop himself. He is changing from black cat to ferocious panther. He springs at the cardinal's throat. He claws his cheeks. He befouls the incense-laden air with his spoor. His hind paws strike Guglielmo in the chest and dislodge him, sending him reeling back against the neat rows of novena candles. Confused, Guglielmo tries to stem the blaze by throwing his cloak over the flames. They are plunged into darkness. The cardinal rises to his feet. His penis dangles flaccidly from his vestments as, making the sign of the cross, he cries out, *"Retro me, Satanas!* I adjure thee and conjure thee, spirit of darkness, to depart from this holy place!"

The vampire laughs bitterly. Through the larynx of the panther, the laugh becomes a roar. The cardinal slinks away toward the vestry. Should he pursue? Should he snuff out this bloated monster? The boy vampire feels only revulsion. The anger was a momentary thing; as it leaves him, he abandons the shape of rage and resolves into the form of the young boy once again.

"Guglielmo," he says softly.

"You came back!" the eunuch whispers. He turns to face him. He has retrieved his cloak from where the molten wax continues to burn a little. Once more there is candlelight, more subdued than before, throwing the chiaroscuro of the painting into even greater relief. "How I longed for you to come back," Guglielmo says. "I've hurt you, and it was only because of envy. I don't want to be immortal any more. I only want to die."

"I can bring that about," says the boy who was once known as Ercolino, chorister in the Sistine Chapel. "If it's what you really want."

For a fleeting moment the deadness leaves Guglielmo's eyes. He is remembering something; what, the boy vampire cannot fathom.

"Yes," he says at last, "I do want it."

He comes forward. He has become pitifully thin. He does not even possess a ghost of his old arrogance, his love of mischief and intrigue. Cardinal del Monte too is a vampire, the boy thinks. They are all vampires, these humans; they feed off one another in ways I cannot even conceive of. If I take his life, what will I give him? Freedom? Is there a hell beyond this hell? The boy vampire cannot know. To endure the torments of hell, it is necessary to have a soul; by his very nature, he is soulless.

Guglielmo loosens his ruff collar and tosses it against the railings. The boy vampire approaches him.

"I'm sorry," he tells him.

Guglielmo is weeping as the fangs, with a pitiless tenderness, pierce through his skin and into his jugular vein. The blood is sour; truly it is laced with opiates and other drugs to numb the awareness of life's bitterness. The boy drinks deep. Blood is blood. His body begins to tingle with the memory of having once lived. The color drains from Guglielmo's face. He grows limp and cold. The boy vampire lays him down upon the altar, beneath the glowering visage of a marble effigy of St. Matthew.

Then he hears a voice from the shadows. "So it was not for me you came, angel of death," says Michelangelo Caravaggio. He steps out from behind a stone pillar.

"Let me finish my work," he says softly. "I don't want him to awaken to eternal loneliness."

Gently, lovingly almost, he rips open the dead eunuch's chest and pulls out his still fibrillating heart. He licks a few last droplets from it as it grows still, and then he places it on the altarcloth, watching the red veins radiate outward from it. He breaks Guglielmo's neck for good measure. He does not want his friend to have to face what he has faced.

Then, wiping the blood from his lips, he turns to Caravaggio. "Thank you for removing me from the painting," he said. "I never belonged there."

"Ah, but I didn't remove you," says the painter. "Look." He points. "You are still there. I only concealed your face. In art, what is not seen is the most beautiful of all."

And the boy looks up, following the curve of the painter's hand, and he sees at last what he should have seen all along; the angel with his face concealed in shadow, leaning down from the sky to bestow on the saint the symbols of his martyrdom.

"There," Caravaggio says, "concealed in the shadow of the crook of your own arm, unreflected in the surface of the cloud, the perfection of your features only hinted at; there you are."

The candlelight flickers. The shadows dance. The shapes of dark and light seem to revolve, to flit across one another. There is life in the picture. Perhaps, in a moment, the angel will look up.

"No," says the boy vampire. "Until we see his face, he has no face. You only think he has my face because once, lost in the labyrinth of your own imagination, you saw me and thought me someone else."

It is true. The angel's face belongs to everyman now. Each man is free to picture it as a reflection of his own yearnings, his secret self. In that sense, it *is* my portrait, thinks the boy. In obeying the cardinal's forbiddance, he has painted me more truly than he himself can know.

"I must go now," he tells Caravaggio.

"Wait! Will you not — for old times' sake — a few quick drops of my blood?"

But the painter speaks to the empty air. Only the art remains.

In the distance, the painter can hear a soft voice, inhumanly sweet and pure, soaring above the music of night: *Miserere mei, miserere mei.*

Only the art....

www.ingramcontent.com/pod-product-compliance
Lightning Source LLC
Chambersburg PA
CBHW040059160426
43192CB00003B/111